Investing in Forex at no cost

WARNING: investing in Forex is risky

The strategies in this book are the result of years of studies and
specializations, so it is not guaranteed the achievement of
same economic results. Past results obtained by the author do not
provide any sort of guarantee for future gains.
The player assumes full responsibility for their own economic choices
financial, aware of the risks connected to any form of
Investment in Forex
The case studies and examples in the text are the result of news and
opinions that can be changed at any time without notice and do not constitute solicitation to buy or sell securities and public savings.
The sole purpose is to provide elements of study on market trends,
therefore they can not be considered as certain and not forecasts
They are unaffected by the risk of the investment transactions.
This book is for informational purposes only and does not want to simulate what is written.

The Author and Publisher assume no responsibility for any inaccuracies
of reported data, damage, economic losses, direct or indirect damages

arising from the use or disclosure of the information
contained in
this book.

- **Introduction**

- **Chapter 1:** What is Forex

- **Chapter 2:** The Basics

- **Chapter 3:** Fundamental Analysis

- **Chapter 4:** Analysis intuitive Technique

- **Chapter 5:** explanation of the strategy with the intuitive technical analysis

- **Chapter 6:** Why use demo

- **Chapter 7:** How to earn without investing a single euro

- **Chapter 8:** Sell Short (Short)

- **Chapter 9:** Swap technique, gain a firm market

- **Chapter 10:** technical terminology and meanings

- **Chapter 11:** Why are important indicators, and when to use them

- **Chapter 12:** Explanations and interpretations of all the most 'used indicators

- **Conclusion**

INTRODUCTION

Many people are fascinated by the world of finance, would like to get in, would like to invest but believe they have adequate skills, and funds, this book is born to these people who would like to invest, then earn while having fun with trading, but without the need to touch their savings, in fact, this book will illustrate 'step by step how the world of Forex, will show you some strategies, and will show' how to earn real money without investing a single euro, and not speaking to you to ask for a loan or ship them to qulche from your friend or relative, but I speak literally invest without getting a single euro.

Many people today with this crisis have ventured into various sectors, sectors for their new and unknown as the Forex.

Why choose Forex?! Simple because the forex is the most 'liquid market in the world (that run much money Katherine about three dollars), and the second reason why it is the most' profitable.

Do not worry even if you've never heard of the Forex and do not know what this book will explain 'everything step by step, and will give' the tools to jump-start your business, complete with a link where to start in a practical way.

If I told you, we play Monopoly, if you lose you lose fake money, but if you win you win real money?! And that's what this book teaches you, invest fake money on the forex to earn real money, this looks like a dream?! Does it seem impossible?! Read on and you'll see that will be 'simple and fun.

- CHAPTER 1 -
What is Forex

The "Forex" or "Foreign exchange market" or simply "FX", is the market in which the exchanges currency in which the operators called "Traders" invest the difference in the exchange of two currencies relationships.

The difference between the stock market and forex are manifold:
The Stock Exchange of securities purchases, which is a very small part of the company, purchasing a very small part of the company 'you determine its trend, in fact, if it were to fail the society' in which you have invested (as it was with Parmalat) you will lose all your capital and it just has nothing.

In the case of Forex this risk is zero, because in order to lose as much money must fail the entire nation.

In Forex we do not buy shares, but we convert our currency into another, and then redo the change when it suits us, I make a practical example:

buying Eur / Usd I convert, the euro dollar, and when I close the position spare dollars into Euros, I told you I close the position and do not sell, because in the field of Forex is not buying stocks you do not sell to earn, but just close your position and automatically enters the gain in your account.

- CHAPTER 2 -
The Basics

Like all financial markets, this market is subject to price fluctuations, and it is this that allows us to win, we can gain is if the market is going up, and if the market goes down '.

In fact there is no crisis in the financial market, there is the market crisis, which sees falling prices, but there is no crisis for a trader, because where the price drops you can 'earn the same due to technical or Short short selling that we will see in later chapters.

The basic concept of Forex, is like that of the substance in the bag, buy when prices are at the minimum, and sell (ie close the position) when the price gets high.

The main difference lies in the so-called volatility,

volatility is the frequency in here moves, I make you a practical example market,
you are observing the currency pair Eur / usd, and see quoted at 1.3223, the price of about one hour is still in the vicinity of the same price, so it means that volatility will be 'low, if the price moves quickly, it means the it is high volatility, in essence volatility is the speed 'in which it moves the price of the currency pair, or action.

- CHAPTER 3 -
Fundamental Analysis

Fundamental Analysis, does not mean an important analysis, but the fundamental analysis in this field is the study of society (in the case of shares) and the study of the nation (in the case of Forex).

It 'important to first fundamental analysis, because it enables us to understand the evolution of the nation, so the currency which is linked to the latter.

There is a fundamental thing you have to know, is called Economic Calendar

Ora	Val.	Impatto	Evento	Attuale	Previsto	Precedente
			Martedì, Luglio 23			
08:45	EUR	▼	Inchiesta congiunturale Francia	95	94	93
10:30	GBP	▼▼	Approvazioni delibere di mutuo BBA	37,3K	38,5K	36,3K
10:45	EUR	▼	Asta Letras Spagnoli 3-Mesi	0,442%		0,869%
13:00	BRL	▼	Indice fiducia consumatori FGV		110,20	112,90
14:30	CAD	▼▼	Vendite al dettaglio (Mensile)		0,4%	0,1%
14:30	CAD	▼▼▼	Vendite al dettaglio beni essenziali (Mensile)		0,1%	-0,3%
14:55	USD	▼	Redbook (Mensile)			0,80%
14:55	USD	▼	Redbook (Annuale)			3,0%
15:00	USD	▼	Indice prezzi abitazioni - USD (Mensile)		0,9%	0,7%
15:00	USD	▼▼	Indice Prezzi delle Case (Annuale)		5,4%	7,4%
15:30	BRL	▼▼	Conto Corrente (USD)		-4,85B	-6,42B
15:30	BRL	▼	Investimenti diretti esteri (USD)		5,50B	3,88B
16:00	USD	▼	Indice FED di Richmond		7	8
16:00	EUR	▼	Fiducia dei consumatori P		-18,3	-18,8
17:30	USD	▼	Asta Buoni Tesoro 4-Settimane			0,020%
17:30	USD	▼	Asta Buoni Tesoro 52-Settimane			0,160%
19:00	USD	▼	Asta Nota Tesoro 2-Anni			0,430%

This is an example of an economic calendar, it will give you 'all the more' important events that may affect the market trend.

If we look closely at the photo, on the 3rd to the left column read (IMPACT) and each event is marked with one, two or three figures depicted with the head of a bull, that is to mean the impact it has that ' event on the performance of that coin, one head, it means that can 'have little impact on the performance of that specific event market, 2 heads, there is important average, while three heads is the maximum, and means you can' have important significance for the market trend.

With fundamental analysis sometimes trading is very simple. Let me give you an example:

When there was the disaster *Fukushima* you who would you have done? Would you have bought their currency? Of course not, in that case such a disaster destroys both shares, Forex, tied to their nation, then you Shorta (that is sold in the open), and you earn when the market goes down, and of course come down 'since the entity 'the damage (the shot or short selling to explain in later chapters).

To trade with fundamental analysis, gives us more

'security, because in these situations it is almost mathematically that the market will fall,

- CHAPTER 4 -
Intuitive Technical Analysis

The intuitive technical analysis is a type of test that is done on the same graph, the latter important if we want to understand the future market trends.

Fundamental analysis leads us to understand how it is going and how it goes' that company, or the country where we choose to invest our money, but obviously it is a type of medium / long-term analysis, to know how to invest, whether long or short, and especially guess the timeing, or (entry time) then we have to rely intuitive technical analysis.

This is a Euro dollar graph, we can see that there are represented several red and green figures, these are called Japanese Candlestick, the green candles Long have meaning, namely that the price has risen to that ace of time while red candles means that the price has dropped.
But every time candle?

Simple, in this case we are in a time frame 5

minutes, then it means that each candle is equivalent to 5 minutes, have the opportunity to set the time at will frame, according to our strategy, in fact, the time frames are of different sizes : time frame: M1, M5, M15, H1, H4, D1, W1, MN,
the M stand for minutes, then M1 = time frame to 1 minute, or every candle is equal to one minute, H stands for now, so in the case of H1 stands for time frame at a time, D1 is for one day or one day , W1 = week, then one week, MN is going to month, or time frame to a month.

Another feature that we must look at is the price, in the picture we can see that right there are numbers, the second number from the top is highlighted in black: 1.35991 means that the euro is quoted at this time 1.35991.

Another important factor is the time on the bottom of the chart, in fact, at the set time frame, below the graph we mostrarà as they scorreremo the days go by.

- CHAPTER 5 -
explanation of the strategy with the intuitive technical analysis

With this section, I do not confine me 'to explain what is intuitive technical analysis, but I'll explain' my strategy, and how do I generate money.

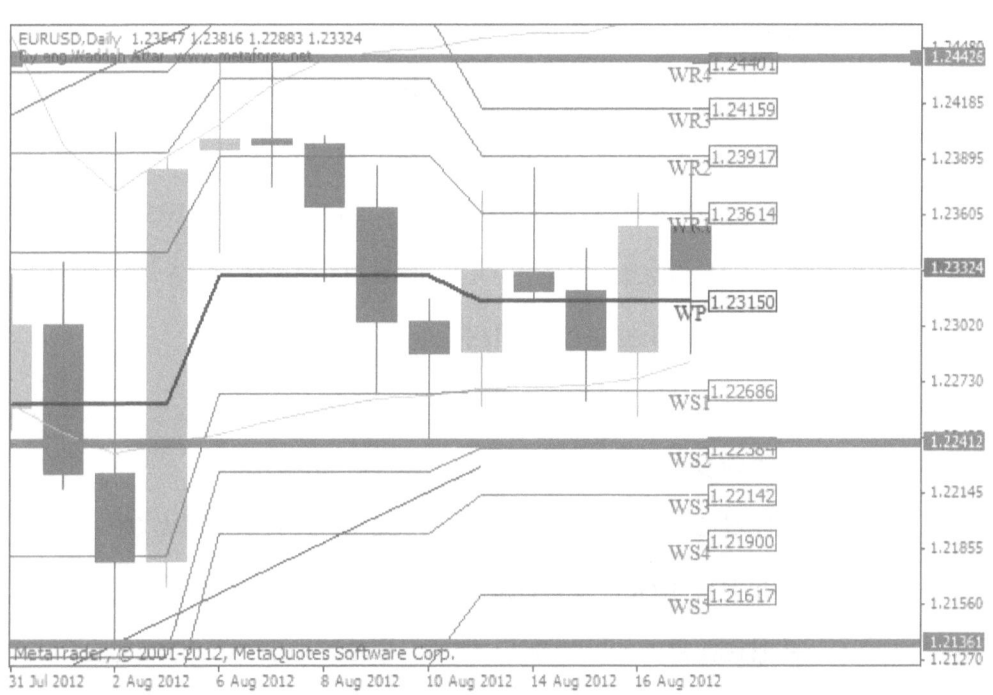

First, we open the graph and verify the support and resistance, for this is an indicator which is called Pivot Point as we can see we have a sequence of horizontal red lines and green, the green lines are the strengths, while the red ones the media, what does it mean ?! With the supports it means that the price at a certain time the ace hit a threshold without going more 'down' but rebounded and rose, so more 'the price bounces off the support and more' it will be 'strong, as well as the resistance, but on the contrary, that the price in a certain period of time, (which we decide through the indicator imostazioni) hit more 'times that price threshold but is not able to overcome it, then he rebounded and it fell.

How to interpret the support and resistance?!
We see in the image that the price is at a height of 1.23324 if the price dovresse past the resistance at 1.23614 then the price will most likely potra 'get up to the next resistance at 1.23917.

After the analysis of support and resistance, let's see if now is the right timing to enter the market, the indicators to be used are: RSI and Stochastic

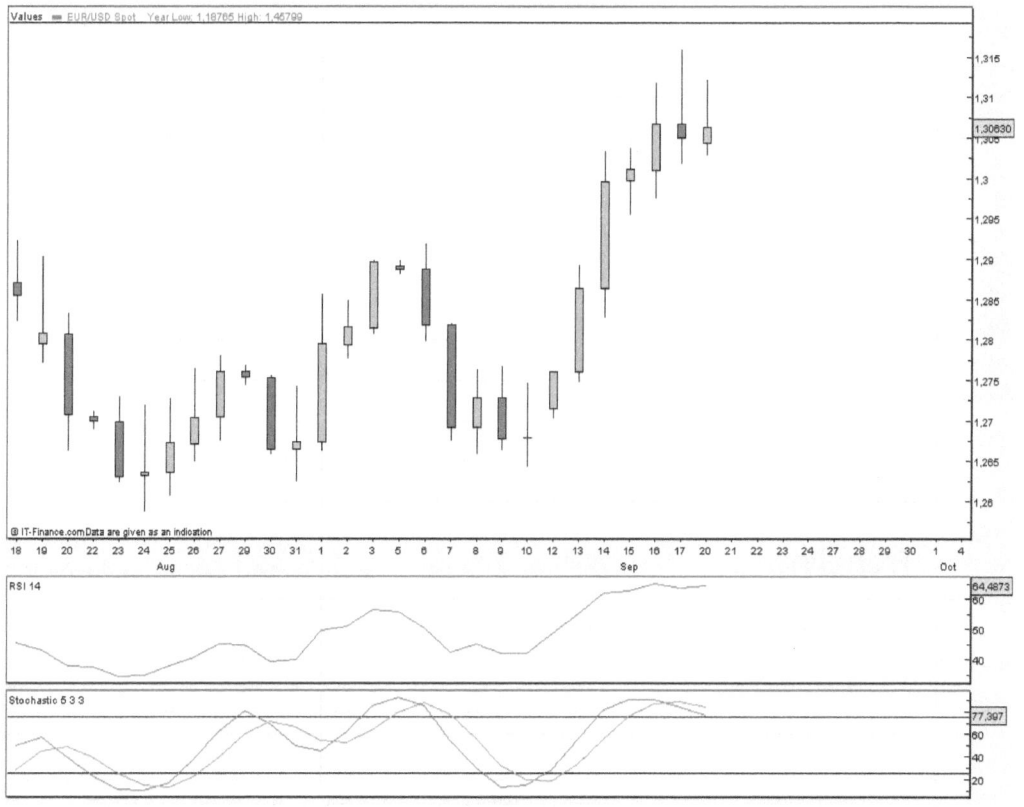

The strategy is very simple, we have to make sure that both indicators are saying the same thing when the RSI indicator is located above the fixed line 60 then it is a short signal, so that we can sell

short because most likely will come down 'the price, when it is below the fixed line 40, then it is a Long signal, because most likely the price will rise '.

To be more precise we see that Stochastic say the same thing
when the two blue and red lines is located above the fixed line 77 and the blue line to the red line to the laundry down then the price could come down, otherwise we have a Long.

Another important thing is to check the performance trend, thanks to the technique Trendline

Let's say all of our indicators give us a long signal, but we are still in a Short trend, then to wait for the exact timeing, draw a line like in the picture, matching the most 'tall candles, and we expect the price pit the trend, as soon as the price pit the trend and indicators give us the current signal, then we begin the operation.

So in summary, to be sure about what to do, whether short or long, and if we get into that time frame, then we must first check:

1. Support and Resistance
2. check if all the indicators give us the same signal
3. verification of the trend

- CHAPTER 6 -
Why use demo

This chapter is to live introduction to this book, if I told you, we play Monopoly, if you lose you lose the Monopoly play money but if you win that money you can convert them into real money, would you like?! Would you like to take risks quadagnare 0 to infinity?! I know it seems impossible seems like a fairy tale, but it's true read on because from now on will reveal 'my secret, which led me to generate money without having invested a single euro.

It is important then use the Demo for 2 reasons:

1. To learn the market, strategies, and platform
2. because we will gain from the demo

you've got it earn the demo, now read my secret in the next chapter

- CHAPTER 7 -
How to earn without investing a single euro

Here we are to live the book, read all the other chapters, where there will also be shown other trading techniques.

You know the Mirror trading?

For those not familiar Mirror trading is nothing more than automatically copy the trading of another trader, and what does this mean?! I make an example

Massimo has a score to Master, while Giulio has a classic trading account, Massimo who knows how the market buys and sells currencies or CFD, while Giulio with its classic trading account is connected to Massimo, so that every time

Massimo open or close 'a position, automatically will open' or close 'position to Julius.

But before explaining how will you gain from all this without spending a euro, you must first understand what are the lots.

What is lot in the Forex?

The lot is the unit that is used to measure the size of the forex transactions.

How much is a STANDARD contract or lot (lot)? On the forex market the size of a standard contract is 100,000 units of the base currency or a batch (lot).

So to operate on the Forex market we need to deposit a minimum of 100,000 units of the base currency account? No, because of the leverage (leverage) used by all brokers we do not need to deposit such as $ 100,000, but only the required margin. S our broker offers us a leverage of 100: 1 (100: 1) we will need 1.000USD, it offers us a 50: 1 leverage we need to deposit 2000USD.

How much is a mini lot (Lot Mini, Mini Forex Contract)?

The value of a mini lot is 1/10 of the standard contract value, then 10,000 units of the base currency with a leverage of 100: 1 and considering that USD the base currency would need only $ 100 to start operating.

How much is a micro lot (micro lot, micro forex contract)?

The micro lot (micro lot) equals 1/100 of a lot or 1/10 of a mini lot then 10000 USD With a 100: 1 leverage would need only $ 10 to start operating.

Table of lot sizes for certain currency pairs

Summarize Standard Lot: 100,000 units of the base currency Mini Lot: 10,000 of the base currency Micro Lot 1,000 units of the base currency

Currency 1.0 lot size 1 pip EURUSD 100,000 EUR 0.0001 USDCHF USD 100,000 0.0001 GBPUSD GBP 70,000 0.0001 USDJPY USD 100.000 00:01

AUDUSD AUD 200,000 0.0001 USDCAD USD 100,000 0.0001 EURCHF 100,000 EUR 0.0001 EURJPY 100,000 EUR 12:01 EURGBP 100,000 EUR 0.0001 GBPJPY GBP 70,000 0:01 GBPCHF GBP 70,000 0.0001 EURCAD EUR 100,000 0.0001 200,000 0.0001 USDSEK NZDUSD NZD USD 100,000 USD 100,000 0.0001 0.0001 USDDKK USDNOK USD 100,000 0.0001 0.0001 USDZAR USDSGD USD 100,000 USD 100,000 100,000 CHF 0.0001 CHFJPY 12:01

Here's how to earn from forex without investing a euro

you'll gain by opening a Master Account, and "selling trading signals" but not literally sell them doing Mirror trading, which will open operations to other people who follow you, then each and every time you open a you position you earn a percentage of them, here is how it works in detail: subscribe to https://www.zulutrade.com, Open an account Master, open the demo, and that's it, every time you open a position, automatically earn 0.5 pips on each lot, whoever follows you, is if you close at a loss if you close both gains in earnings always !!! obviously if you start to lose slowly your followers they will go, so I recommend you apply and do more 'winning trades possible, so he can consistently earn, you earn 100, 1,000, 3,000 euro per transaction, and even more' , depend 'on you

- CHAPTER 8 -
Sell Short (Short)

I know you will do early difficulty 'to sell out if you have not bought anything, because we are used to sell when we bought something, then we sell something that we bought, the market works differently, I'll explain in a clear and simple, because many on the internet explain it in a way too technical, and who is novice does not understand it.

If the Buy, we earn when it is the dollar's position on the euro, the price rises, whereas in the case of Short (short selling) we earn when it drops.

To sell short we have no action, or open position, just click Short, and will automatically open 'position in Short, so when the gain goes down the market.

Here's how it works technically

In the case of shares, us when we sell the open users in Buy those actions, they shall give, then we buy them when they are more 'lower than we bought, the shares returned to them, and profit us ,
 the same is true for the Forex, but instead, are they Forex contracts

- CHAPTER 9 -
Technical Swap, gain a firm market

There are days when the market is at a standstill, no trend, and we have a sideways market, namely, the market walking in a range without exceeding the resistance is above, and that support beneath, so without giving us the opportunity 'to money with long and short, what we do in these cases, we wait?! Yeah, or we could use the SWAP technique, the swap is un'interesse, or a subtraction on our capital, depending on the Buy / Sell position.

I make an example:

With € 3,000 buy Eur / Usd buying this pair give us about $ 20 each day, so if we open the position for 22 to 23 we pay the interest, and so at 23 the next day, until we cap it off, so if we know that will last 'sideways market for 3 days, we will gain only holding open the location in Long, thanks to the SWAP.

The swaps are different from each Broker This is the list of one of the most 'known Broker in London

AUDUSD	0:49 pips	-0.76 pips
EURCHF	0:02 pips	-0.07 pips
EURGBP	-0.16 pips	0:05 pips
EURJPY	0:03 pips	-0.03 pips
EURUSD	-0.04 pips	0:01 pips
GBPUSD	0:08 pips	-0.19 pips
NZDUSD	0:42 pips	-0.65 pips
USDCAD	-0.31 pips	0:14 pips
USDCHF	0:17 pips	-0.11 pips
USDJPY	0:01 pips	-0.04 pips

AUDCAD	0:28 pips	-0.55 pips
AUDCHF	0:45 pips	-0.75 pips
AUDJPY	0:50 pips	-0.75 pips
CADCHF	0.1 pips	-0.39 pips
CADJPY	0:11 pips	-0.37 pips
CHFJPY	-0.01 pips	0 pips
EURAUD	-1.19 pips	0.79 pips
EURCAD	-0.43 pips	0.2 pips

GBPAUD	-1.24 pips	0.99 pips
GBPCAD	-0.47 pips	0:24 pips
GBPCHF	-0.05 pips	-0.25 pips
GBPTRY	-10.37 pips	6.6 pips
GBPJPY	-0.04 pips	-0.17 pips
NZDCAD	0:23 pips	-0.47 pips
NZDCHF	0:39 pips	-0.64 pips
NZDJPY	0:42 pips	-0.64 pips
SGDJPY	0:01 pips	-0.1 pips
USDHKD	0:08 pips	-0.16 pips
USDSGD	0 pips	-0.04 pips

AUDNZD	-0.06 pips	0 pips
EURDKK	-1.41 pips	-0.63 pips
EURHUF	-3.26 pips	1.96 pips
EURNOK	-4.48 pips	24.2 pips
EURNZD	-1.32 pips	0.87 pips
EURSEK	-3.44 pips	1.7 pips
EURSGD	-0.23 pips	-0.23 pips
EURTRY	-8.8 pips	27.5 pips
GBPNZD	-1.36 pips	1.9 pips
TRYJPY	0.81 pips	-1.35 pips
USDBRL	-5.57 pips	23.3 pips
USDDKK	-1 pips	-0.57 pips
USDCNH	-1.18 pips	0:17 pips
USDHUF	-2.38 pips	1:44 pips
USDMXN	-15.3 pips	11:54 pips
USDNOK	-3.26 pips	1:53 pips
USDSEK	-2.49 pips	0.66 pips
USDTRY	-6.49 pips	3:47 pips
USDZAR	-14.17 pips	11.3 pips

GOLD	-1.45 pips	-0.52 pips
SILVER	-1.2 pips	-0.43 pips

PLATINUM	-1.53 pips	-0.55 pips
PALLADIUM	-0.79 pips	-0.28 pips

- CHAPTER 10 -
technical terminology and meanings

Base currency The "base currency" is the first currency that makes up a pair, the one that remains constant (eg. If the pair is the EUR / USD the "base currency" is the Euro). The euro, in fact, is for Europe's dominant currency basis. As a result, currency pairs against the Euro will be identified as EUR / USD, EUR / GBP, EUR / CHF, EUR / JPY, EUR / CAD, etc. The British Pound is the next base currency used in the hierarchy. The major pairs against the GBP are identified as GBP / USD, GBP / CHF, GBP / JPY, GBP / CAD.

Bear Market - Market declining market in which prices fall rapidly, due to the general pessimism (opposite the market rising "Bull.")

Bid - Question Price that the buyer is willing to pay to buy; price offered for a currency.

Balance of payments The registration of all transitions between a country and the rest of the world; It includes information on the value of trade in goods and services and on the value of the transfers.

Bull Market - In hike Market characterized by rising prices.

Break Even Point (Bep, breakeven point) Unit of time or production volume at which the revenues derived from an investment equals the costs incurred.

Forex Broker Intermediary that is the purchase or sale instructions of investors' currencies and transmits them to the market, thereby providing the service that allows physically carrying out trading activity.

CCable slang name given to cross Sterling / Dollar amerciano.

Call Rate - Rate Money Market interbank interest rate daily.

Cash flow Cash flow generated by a company cash in a given period of time available for new investments or capital employed.

Central bank It is the main monetary authorities of each country, controlled by the central government. And 'responsible for the issuance of currency, monetary policy, interest rates, and the regulation and supervision of the banking private sector. The Federal Reserve (Fed) is the central bank for the United States. In Europe we have the European Central Bank (ECB) and in Japan there is the Bank of Japan (BOJ).

Cash Market - Cash Market Market immediate purchases and sales of currencies.

Cross Rate - cross Courses The exchange rates between two currencies generally obtained from the exchange rates of individual interest of the two currencies measured by the US dollar.

Currency Risk - risk of exchange rates Risk of suffering losses in case of inverse exchange rates change.

Currency Swap - Currency Changes Contact who hires the two parties to change the interest payment flows in different currencies, for a period of time mutually agreed and to change the main completed in different currencies at a pre-specified interest rate.

D

Day Trading Open and close the position - or the same positions - in one meeting. Public debt The total value of debts not yet repaid by the public administration contracts.

Deflation general decrease in the price level, that is, a negative inflation. **Devaluation (devaluation)** Decreasing the unavaluta value than the value of the currency of another country. When a country devalues its currency, the goods that are imported become more expensive, while the goods that are exported are less expensive and thus more competitive.

Dollar Rate - Dollar Rates a foreign currency variable amount listed for a difference between the dollar regardless of the place of residence of the negotiator or the currency you want to invest. The only exception is the sterling exchange rate / US Dollar (cable) which is quoted as variable amount in dollars against sterling.

Dumping The sale of assets by foreign companies at a price below the unit cost, or lower than the price charged in the country they belong to those entities.

IS

EMS - EMS Abbreviation for European Monetary systems: agreed with the European Union member countries to maintain alignment between the exchange rates of their respective currencies.

Federal Reserve (Fed) Central Bank of the Member-States.

Fixed Exchange Rate - Courses of fixed exchange rates Official rate set by monetary authorities for one or more currencies. In practice, even fixed courses may be subject to fluctuations between high and low pre-established previously, requiring an appropriate intervention.

Flat / Square - Square equilibrium position. A notebook is balanced if negotiation does not have any position or any position they cancel each other.

Foreign Exchange Swap - Changes in exchange rates. Transaction which involves the actual exchange of two specific dates between two currencies (main) - a date with the rates determined at the time of conclusion of the contract ("short leg"), and a date in the longer term with a set at the time rate the contract is signed.

Ou ou FX Foreign Exchange Forex - Currency Currency The purchase of one currency simultaneously with the sale of another in non-exchange Most of the FX operations are calculated in relation to the US dollar. **Fundamental Analysis - Fundamental Analysis** in-depth analysis of the economic and commercial data in order to determine the future evolution of the financial markets.

GTC - valid until revoked Order to a counterparty to buy or sell at a fixed price. This order is valid until it is canceled by the customer.

H

Hedging - Hedging Practice which states to 'engage in investment activities in order to cover the losses of another, for example by selling to hedge to offset a previous purchase or buy to cover to make a sale to cover. Although hedges reduce potential losses, they also tend to limit the potential profits.

Hedge fund a private investment fund, designed for investors who have large capital (generally the minimum investment is $ 1 million) and specialized in short-term high-risk speculation. The hedge funds operate on bonds, currencies, stock options and derivatives.

High / Low - High / Low Normally, the price negotiated higher or lower for sottogiacente instrument during the current session.

Holding Company that owns and manages investments in other companies for the purpose of monitoring their activities or make profits.

Home Banking Service that allows customers to connect via the Internet to their bank (thus also from home, hence the name) and make your PC from various operations, such as the consultation of bank accounts, paying bills, buying stocks.

THE

If done Type correlation between orders; the execution of an order is conditional upon the occurrence of another order.

Inflation Increase in the general price level.

Interbank Interbank market.

Initial Margin - Initial Margin initial guarantee deposit required to enter a position, and that serves as insurance for future executions.

Interbank Rates - Interbank rate Tasi exchange to which large international banks quote other large international banks.

Joint Venture Collaboration between two or more companies for the construction of a common project, which involves the synergistic use of resources.

LeverageLeverage (leverage): Financial leverage is to maneuver a certain amount using a minimal capital investment. In other words, one could say that exploit leverage, in essence, it means borrow capital trusting in his own ability to invest obtaining a higher yield. (Es.- using a capital of 10,000 euros, leveraged 10, gains or losses will be recognized on an amount of 100,000 Euro.). A movement on the chosen currency pair, example Euro / Dollar, equal to 1% will result, using a lever 10, a variation of the investment equal to 10%.

Limit Order - Order to limited progress Order

to buy at a price lower than or equal to a specified amount, or to sell at a price equal to or greater than an amount specified.

Long Position - Long position covering Market position where the client has bought a currency he previously absent. Normally expressed as a function of the currency, eg dollars long (short marks).

Margin - Margin Customers must deposit as collateral for funds to cover potential losses due to adverse movement in quotations. Margin Call - Margin Call Request for additional funds. Condition imposed by a clearing house to a member (or a clearing firm to a client) to make a minimum deposit to cover an adverse movement in prices in the market. Particular conformation of calndlestic graphics characterized by a single candle devoid of "shadows" or "tails".

Offer - Offer The price or rate, at which a potential

seller is ready to sell. detailed order in which the execution of an order automatically cancels the other game. **Open Position - Position open**Market that has not been regulated by a material payment or was not reversed by another equal or opposite the market for the same date adjustment.

PIPA term used in the exchange market to represent the smallest increment possible for an exchange rate. According to the context, this value is equal to a base point (0.0001 in the case of pairs EUR / USD, GBD / USD, and 0.01 in the pairs USD / JPY - EUR / JPY).

Resistance - Resistance Threshold for which there is a tendency for sale. **Risk Capital - Capital at risk** Amount of money that a person can afford to invest and whose loss will not affect your standard of living. **Rollover - Reconciliation** when the settlement of a transaction can be traced back to another date-dependent control of the interest rate differential of the two currencies.

Short - Sale to cover Selling to hedge means selling an instrument without actually owning it, and hold a covering position waiting for the fall of the course so that the instrument can be purchased later at a profit. **Spot - Operation in contant**Transaction carried out immediately even though the funds generally only change hands within two days after the conclusion of the market.

Spread - Scrap The difference between the supply and demand (selling price); It used to measure market liquidity. Waste limited usually indicate a great fluidity.**Stop Loss Order - stop order** An order to buy or sell in the market when the price reaches the set threshold, is below that recorded during the above at the time of the order.

Technical Analysis - Technical Analysis Analysis that strives to predict the future evolution of the market by examining market data as graphs, of course and volume trends.

Value Date - Value date Date Currency contracts in cash or deferred delivery.

Leverage: Using margin to operate with more capital. In the currency market, leverage is almost always displayed as a percentage. For example: 1% margin produces a leverage 100: 1, therefore, a deposit of $ 10,000 will have the ability to hold open positions for a value of $ 1,000,000 (ie 100 times higher).

Expert Advisior: Script (or automatic procedure) capable of providing help to the trader (or even operate autonomously) in financial trades. Fund: term used by brokers to indicate the "cash payment" operation on the Forex account

Gap: Missing distance between the closing price and opening new market. It notices a gap when the price jumps on their own scale of values.

Hedging: option to cover one or more positions with offsetting positions in order to reduce the investment risk

Leverage: Lever (or leverage). Multiplier the invested capital which allows only invest a guarantee margin with respect to the total investment value.

Long: open position for purchase (buy). In English it says: go "Long"

Margin: Amount of money that must be available on the Forex account and which necessarily must have "to ensure against leakage" of open positions. The initial margin must be available on the account before opening a new position. The margin of "maintenance" may be added to the initial margin with subsequent payments.

Margin Call: Request for additional funds by the Broker in order to "cover" losses already in place on open positions. In the absence of the required margin, the trader has the real risk that its positions are closed in partially or totally at the discretion of the Broker due to insufficient funds.

overnight: negotiation that remains open until the

next day.

Trading Platform: (In English Trading Platform) software that allows you to make transactions in the market.

pip: is an acronym which stands for "Percentage In Point". It is the smallest unit of a Forex price.

Resistance: Price threshold where sellers are reverse trend to a rising market.

Rollover: Closing a negotiation postponed forward on another date which implies a cost based on the differential rate of the two currencies.

Short: position open for sale (sell). In English it says go "Short".

Slippage: deviation of the price of the order to trade and the actual market price

spread: price difference between the application (Ask) and bid (Bid)

Spread Trading: trading operation carried out

simultaneously on various financial instruments to reduce its exposure to market risk.

Stop loss: price level at which the position is liquid even at a loss, with the objective to protect itself from further market movements contrary to the direction of their trade.

Stop profit (or TakeProfit): Executed order to cash the gain of a profitable operation.

Support: Price threshold where buyers are reversing trend to a downward market.

Target profit (TP): Price threshold where the investor thinks of having to close an operation.

Tick: the slightest movement of the price of a listed instrument.

TimeFrame: period of observation of quotes (eg. 30min / 1h / 4h)

Trend: Trend, market direction

withdraw: term used by brokers to indicate the operation of "taking money" from the Forex account

- CHAPTER 11 -

Why are important indicators, and when to use them

If you're here it means that you, like many other traders, have set themselves an important question and clever: why are they important the trading indicators? The answer of course is very detailed and it also becomes difficult to objectively assess because there are conflicting opinions about it. But we can draw a line connecting common thought a bit 'all experienced traders. First of all try to understand what are the indicators and what they are.

WHAT ARE THE INDICATORS OF TRADING

The trading indicators are graphical representations that are based on well-defined parameters that refer to the market price of a particular financial instrument. Thanks to the indicators we can get an idea of what is happening in the market at any given time. Let's clarify a concept well, the indicators do not help to predict the market, the indicators give us an overview and make us figure out where to move prices and as hard as they do. In this regard, we can say that in principle there are many indicators which, although different, say the same thing using different languages and, therefore, different graphical representations.

Nevertheless, the best indicator, according to many traders, is the price. This means that nothing can ever replace the Price Analysis understood as analysis of trends and areas of support and resistance. Associated with this analysis should also be made a careful analysis of trading volumes, which in the forex market, however, are related to the broker to which we refer and not to the entire market. This factor is not negligible because the volume that we see does not represent all the investment, but only the sum of those traders who uses or our brokers are doing the same.

WHEN TRUST OF INDICATORS

An indicator turns out to be reliable if the signal that gives us and can be confirmed by our analysis and by another indicator. This means that the indicators are prone to false signals that can compromise our analysis and must therefore be avoided. Each indicator should be confirmed by another and these, together, are to be compared with our analysis. Ultimately, the indicators represent an extremely valuable trading tool that should be used, but with due caution and had attitude, as we have always stated, must be detached and rational.

- CHAPTER 12 -
Explanations and interpretations of all the most 'used indicators

PRICE

The indicators there are so infinite 'I am going to show you it' s just the most 'known and most' important.

The price is the price trend.
It can be presented in various forms (curve, bar chart, candles, mountain, histogram).
You can change the style of a slideshow by clicking the right mouse button on the price. Select 'Properties Price' or click on the wrench icon located on the top left in the title of 'indicator. Select the desired presentation style.
practical aspect:
In order to achieve more effective analysis, we recommend working in bar chart or candles. This

will allow you to get the most information (open, high, low, close) for each period studied.

Moving Average (On the price)

Moving Average

Definition:

Simple Moving Average = (ChiusuraAttuale ChiusuraGiornoPrecedente + + .. Closing ([X-1] th previous day) / X.

X is the parameter determining the number of days to be considered in the calculation.

The Exponential Moving Average gives a stronger weighting to the latest quotes and so reacts more strongly to recent changes in price. The exponential moving average is obtained in the following manner. It is calculated in a first time the exponential% = 2 / (period + 1). The exponential moving average translates to (closing the day * exponenziale%) + (Moving Average Eve * (100-% exponenziale))

The triangular moving average corresponds to a simple moving average on which is necessary to apply a double smoothing. The weighted moving average is calculated in the following manner $MMP = (P_1 C_t + P_2 C_{(t-1)} + \ldots + P_n C_{(t_n)}) / (P_1 + P_2 + \ldots + P_n)$, being P the weight and C_t pricing at the time t.

Interpretation:

A moving average is an average price agreement on the period considered.

So moving averages are useful to highlight trends. 0 Put the box to not display the moving average corrispondente.Quando a shorter moving average crosses above the long moving average the trend become bullish and each other when the short term moving average crosses below the long moving average the trend becomes bearish. You can also use a single medium acting on the junctions with the listing of the value.

Volume

Definition:

The volume is given by the total shares traded during the selected time frame (day, week, Intraday ..)

Interpretation:
It may indicate the strength of the variation in progress and the emotionality of investors.

practical aspect:
A valid uptrend is accompanied by large volumes, and in the growth of the weaker volumes on corrections of this increase.
Conversely, a valid bearish trend is accompanied by important volumes on declines and weaker volumes about fixes.

Tip:
You can 'draw a moving average on x days.
To add a moving average (or other) to an indicator, you need to click on the wrench located on the top left in the indicator window concerned. Therefore, a window will appear; select the function (add) status, and subsequently the desired indicator (eg

moving average)

Volume

accumulation

Definition:
sum [volume * ((Closing-current cheapest) - (PiuAlto-Closing)) / (PiuAlto-current cheapest)].
Interpretation:
This indicator weighs volumes using the closing price compared to the extreme points of the day. It validates the ongoing movement evolving in the same direction of stock prices. A divergence between the quotes and the Accumulation / Distribution is often an inversion signal of the current trend.
practical aspect:
These volume oscillators can be very useful for determining the accumulation stages or distribution.

ADX, ADXR

Definition:

It first calculates + DM and -DM that represent the directional movement, ie the number of points earned in a given direction. It applies later smoothing Wilder of + DM et -DM to calculate + DI -DI et. It then calculates the DX.
Dx = 100 * ((+ DI) - (- DI)) / ((A +) + (- DI)).
To finalize the calculation applies a smoothing Wilder on DX.

Interpretation:

DI + represents a buying pressure et DI- selling pressure.
When DI +> DI- a buy signal can be given and the same way when DI-DI + <can be given a sell signal.
The ADX and ADXR are two indicators of movement indicators.
A trend can be placed in relief when ADX or ADXR are higher than 17 or 23.

Instead, if ADX and ADXR are less than 17 or 23, the market does not present any trend.

The ADX and ADXR crossings allow to determine the inputs and outputs signals.

practical aspect:

When ADX ADXR ou are above the threshold of 17 or 23, the market is in a trend, a buy or sell signal is given by the intersection of DI + DI-et.

When ADX and ADXR pass under the threshold of 17 or 23, the market has no trend. We suggest in this case to exit the market.

Equally, it is best to take profits when AXD crosses ADXR downward since the market trend ends.

Aroon

Definition:

For a given period of x days:

- Aroon Up is the number of days the maximum period.

- Aroon Down is the number of days since the last minimum.

These indicators are comprised between 0 and 100. For example, if the price is currently higher in the new period of x days considered, the Aroon Up = 100; if the price was the highest at the beginning of the period, the Aroon Up = 0.

Interpretation:
This indicator can help reveal trends.
A Aroon Up high (above 70) indicates a bullish atendenza.
A Aroon Down low (under 30) is revealing of a bullish trend.
A low Aroon Up and Aroon Down higher indicate a downward trend.
practical aspect:
Parallel evolution dell'Aroon Up and Down is often associated with a consolidation trend.
Conversely, a cross is a sign:
-When the dell'Aroon Down line crosses upward the dell'Aroon Up, you can expect a future downward.
-When dell'Aroon up the line crosses the dell'Aroon down we can expect a rise in the future.

Average True Range

Definition:

The True Range and Average True Range allow to represent the volatility of a value

The true range is the highest value in absolute value between:

(Piualto day - the current cheapest day)

(Piualto day - closing Eve)

(Current cheapest day - closing Eve)

To calculate the AverageTrue Range, you have to apply a moving average of the True Range.

Interpretation:

This volatility indicator determines the pressure of sellers and acquirenti.Cosi a high ATR will mean a strong pressure and therefore have a strong value volatility.

Reciprocally a weak ATR will mean a weak pressure and hence low volatility.

practical aspect:

A spike sull'ATR often translates a market panic accompanied by a major marketing move.

Bollinger Bands

Definition:
Indicator = (upper band - lower band) / Media Mobile.
Interpretation:
This indicator is calculated from the Bollinger bands.
It allows you to see if the bands are forming a bubble or not.
So you can determine the power of the market trend.
If the indicator is growing, the market enters a trend and another indicator shows a decline deflation trend, the trend decellera.
In a market without trend, you will notice that the Bollinger bands will be able to serve as a support resistances.

Bollinger BandWidth

Definition:

The Bollinger Bands are bands based on a moving average at a distance of n standard deviations.

They are composed of 2 parameters:

the period

the number of waste-type. n

Interpretation:

Bollinger bands will automatically adjust depending on market volatility.

So 95% of the quotations must be within the bands if it is assumed that prices follow a normal law.

practical aspect:

Bands must be strong areas of support and resistance when the market is no trend.

When the gap between the two bands decreases after having increased, the tendency fades.

Chaikin's Money Flow

Definition:

E 'calculated from the indicator Accumulation / Distribution. The parameter is the number of days used in the formula. The calculation in histogram mode is identical to the line way.

Interpretation:
It indicates the buying and selling pressure.
When the money flow remains largely above 0, it indicates a buying pressure and vice versa. This indicator can be used starting from differences.

practical aspect:
A bearish reversal may flash when a bearish divergence appears. It is obtained when the curve of prices touching a new higher while the indicator remains below its previous high point.
A bullish reversal may flash when a bullish divergence appears. It is obtained when the price makes a new low while the indicator remains above its previous low point.

Chaikin's Volatility

Definition:

The Chaikin Volatility is obtained by calculating the exponential moving average of the difference between the maximum and the minimum of the day and calculating the percentage of variation of this moving average. The parameters are the number of days considered to calculate the moving average and the rate of change.

Interpretation:

The volatility of Chaikin compares the difference between the highest price and the lowest price of a title. A high volatility is the maturity index of a peak while a low volatility represents a basic level.

Chande kroll stop (On the price)

Definition:
Stop preliminary high = HIGHEST [p] (high) - x * Average True Range [p]
Stop preliminary bottom = LOWEST [p] (high) + x

* Average True Range [p]

Stop short = HIGHEST [q] (preliminary top stop)

Stop long = LOWEST [q] (bass preliminary stop)

Interpretation:

The Chande Kroll Stop Indicator is a tool that indicates the levels of the respective stop for long or short positions. It is calibrated to the true range which makes it independent of the volatility of the securities. This means that the preliminary stop are situated below the highest (or above the lowest) of 'p' latest bars, the standard deviation being proportional to the average True Range on 'p' bars. The stop appearing on the graph can be deduced by taking respectively the highest and the lowest of the preliminary stop on the 'q' latest bars.

And 'possible to place a buy stop on breaking the upper band, and a sell stop on breaking the lower band.

Chande momentum oscillator

Definition:

Pos = positive part of the quotations variation (a value of 0, if the variation of the prices is negative)
Neg = negative part of the quotes of variation (that is 0 if the variation of the prices is positive)
At every moment, the change in prices is therefore valid: Pos - Neg
They calculate simple moving averages ap days of Pos Neg et notice MPos and Mneg
Chande Momentum Oscillator = (MPos - Mneg) / (+ MPos Mneg) * 100

Interpretation:
This indicator like RSI is presented on a limited scale between -100 et +100. When the indicator is the threshold +50, there is a sovraccquisto and mutually when the indicator is <-50 the threshold, there is a sopravendita. The indicator can be smoothed by a moving average. How about a RSI

is two moving averages can use it by applying that serve as points of entry and exit when they present themselves to the crossroads. E 'equally possible to intervene on this indicator tracing the lines of support and resistance but equally looking classic chartiste configurations (dual vertex etc ....). The study of differences is equally used. Recall:

You get a bullish divergence when the price makes a new low while the indicator remains below its previous low.

You get a bearish divergence when the price makes a new high and the indicator remains below its previous high.

Cycle - Cycle

Definition:
To build the cycle indicator, we begin to build the following indicator:

$I = [4.1 * \text{Stochastic\% K}(5.3) + 2.5 * \text{Stochastic\% K}(14.3) + \text{Stochastic\% K}(45.14) + 4 * \text{Stochastic\% K}$

(75.20)] / 11.6

Then it calculates the simple moving average from I to 9 bars.

mm = Average [9] (I) Finally, the cycle indicator is the difference between these two quantities: Cycle = I - mm

Interpretation:

In the current life cycles allow us to predict the events:

For example (the tides, planetary movements, seasons etc ...).

The analysis of the cycles is also used in financial markets to determine the trend reversals.
Depending on these cycles can be inserted and removed more easily your positions.
This analysis is interesting on commodity markets mainly related to the seasons.
For the values related to these redundant natural phenomena, it is called cyclic values.

CCI - Commodity Channel Index

Definition:

The CCI calculates the difference between the listing and its average on the 'x' days reported in 1.5% of the gap-type.

$CCI = (M-MM) / (0.015 * D)$

$M = (H + L + c) / 3$

MM = moving average from an M days

H: higher

L: lower

C: Closing

D: standard deviation from the average.

Interpretation:

The CCI icon corresponds to the variation in prices compared to their statistical average.

It 'a market speedometer that gives indications of sovraccquisto (CCI> 100) and sopravendita (CCI <- 100).

A divergence with the price of the securities announces a future market correction.

DEMA - Double Exponential Moving Average:

Definition:

It is calculated in a first time the MME1, an exponential moving average days on the closing prices.

Afterwards it calculates the MME2, the moving average of days an exponential MME1.

He finally gets the indicator DEMA = 2 * MME1 - MME2

Interpretation:

This indicator is faster and smoother than a standard moving average. The Demas can be used in place of moving averages or applied on other indicators such as the MACD or stochastic oscillators

DPO - Detrended Price Oscillator:

Definition:

Calculation of a DPO for the period n.

You get the DPO by calculating an arithmetic moving average of period n on the closing prices. You have to back off the data from this average of (n / 2 + 1) days back.

The DPO indicator is finally obtained by: listing of each closure - listing of each value of the moving average shifted).

Interpretation:

The DPO indicator minimizes the tendency of prices.

Mette so highlight the cycles of a period less than the period 'n' chosen (points of entry and exit points).

Browsing the peaks and troughs in the DPO puts the value of the value cycles.

Directional Movement

DI - Directional Indicator
Definition:

DI + = + DM / TR; DI- = DM / TR In stogramma way, the bars represent DI + DI- with less

TR = max [abs (PiuAlto-current cheapest); abs (PiuAlto-ChiusuraVigilia); abs (current cheapest-ChiusuraVigilia)]

DM + = max [0; PiùAlto-PiuAltoVigilia]

DM = max [0; PiuBassoVigilia-current cheapest]

The parameter determines the number of days considered that smooth the two lines with the help of the method of moving averages

In histogram mode, the bars represent less DI + DI-

Interpretation:

The + DI measures the upward movement. The DI- measures the bearish movements.

A buy signal may appear when DI + crosses upward DI- and a sell signal may appear when DI + crosses DI- downward.

practical aspect:

To validate the purchase and sale signals during

the DI + and DI- crossings, it is necessary that the trend is identified, in particular with a high ADX (greater than a certain threshold, for example 17 or 23).

Ease Of Movement - Easy Movement

Definition:

A = Maximum

B = Minimum

A day before the previous day = max

B previous day = minimum of the previous day

V = Volume

EMV = 0.5 * (A + B - + Avigilia Bvigilia) / [v / (HB)]

Interpretation:

This indicator allows to characterize a market that does not require large volumes for prices to change.

Surely, a positive value dell'EMV results in a bull market, a negative value in a downturn.

Of the values indicate a long way from 0 associated with small volumes of the bull market orientation or downward (the market has ease of movement). Conversely, if prices need large volumes to change or if the prices almost do not move, the EMV will be close to 0.

practical aspect:

If the EMV exceeds the line 0, it can launch a buy signal and mutually when the EMV passes under the 0 line, can possibly launch a sell signal.

ElderRay

Definition:

The Elder-Ray is composed of two indicators: the Bull Power and Bear Power.

The Bull Power corresponds to the distance between the highest of the current bar and an exponential moving average.

Interpretation:

The Bull Power represents the capacity of bullish (i 'Bulls' ie the 'bulls') to push prices above the average consensus. And 'when growing bullish exert increasing pressure on prices, decreasing when you weaken.

The 'Bear power' shows the ability of the bears (i'Bears', ie the 'bears') to push prices below the average consensus of the title. The indicator is decreasing when the bears are stronger. The 'bear power' is generally negative, it becomes a positive means that the bulls have regained control.

A Bull Power negative results a great weakness of the bulls.

Enveloppes

Definition:
The principle of the calculation is simple, it is of an arithmetic moving average of an n period applied to the closing.
The upper band is obtained by adding a percentage% compared to the data of this moving

average.

Similarly, the lower band is obtained by subtracting this same percentage% compared to the data of this moving average.

Interpretation:
The lower and upper bands serve as support and resistance according to the same principle of Bollinger bands in a market without trend.

Error type

Definition:
The Error type lets you know if share prices analyzed approach the regression line; more quotes come close to the straight line and the trend is reliable.
On the contrary more quotations is alllontanano by the straight line of linear regression and less reliable is the trend.

practical aspect:

This indicator is often linked all'R2 easier to interpret a trend reversal.

When the two indicators depart from opposite levels and then converge, it is often observed a trend reversal, or a new phase of consolidation and possibly capsizing.

Force Index

Definition:

Force Index = (ending date (day) -closing (Eve)) * Volume.

Interpretation:

This indicator measures the strength of buyers and sellers ('Bulls' e'Bears').

If the closing price is higher than the previous day, the force will be positive (negative inversely).

The Intensity of the force will depend on the

importance of the volumes at stake.

practical aspect:

Force A positive index means that the market is dominated by buyers, while Force Index negative signals the dominance of sellers.

A divergence of Force Index and price developments is a sign:

-d'acquisto if the stock price reaches a minimum while the Force Index indicator remains below its previous low.

-to sell if the price makes a new high while Force Index indicator remains below its previous high (bearish divergence)

historical volatility

Historical Volatility

Definition:

To calculate this indicator, you must first choose the period (eg 20 days utime).

Then they calculate the variations of each day of this period.

Then it calculates the logarithm neperiano then the variance of this set of values.

By extrapolation we get the historical volatility as a percentage.

Interpretation:

When volatility is important trend changes can take place both upward and downward.

Ichimoku (On the price)

The Ichimoku study consists of 4 lines calculated in the following way: / n / n1. Tenkan-Sen or conversion line = (max + min) / 2, during the last periods p1; / n / n2. Kijun-Sen or baseline = (max + min) / 2, during the past p2 periods; / n / n3. Senkou Span A or main extension A = (Tenkan-Sen

+ Kijun-Sen) / 2, delayed by p4 previous periods; / n / n4. Senkou Span B or main extension B = (maximum + minimum) / 2, during the last periods p3, p4 on delayed periods precedenti./n/nI default values are p1 = 9, p2 = 26, p3 = 53, p4 = 26 ./n/n/nIl Kumo or cloud is the area between the Senkou A and B./n/nIl sell signal is generated when the Tenkan-Sen crosses the Kijun-Sen from above. / n / nI Kumo or the clouds serve as areas of support / resistance and help identify trends. When the price is above the clouds, the trend is bullish. When it is below the trend is bearish.

Line Indicator Horizontal

Definition:

The horizontal line is very interesting because it allows you to place the lower and upper limits on the indicators they will use.

practical aspect:

You can also use the alarms to know through an audible and / or visual alarm when the indicator exceeds the upward and downward the level that you have drawn. It should be noted that the horizontal lines are already present on many indicators (RSI, Stochastic, ….).

dynamic horizontal line

Interpretation:

You know the location of the latest price. QPermette, therefore, to know whether it is possibly a support or a resistance. It will, therefore, if the prices are close to the strategic points (the point of reverse, accumulation zone). In the window (Property Prices) can also apply this line of different prices (closed, open, high, low …).

Vertical Line (On the price)

Interpretation:

The vertical line allows to place a reference along the price curve and know the position of a rod to a configurable number of previous periods.

Unlike object 'vertical line' which allows to delimit a period that evolves over time, this line allows to delimit a fixed period directly on the price chart.

MACD - Moving Average Convergence Divergence

Definition:
The blue line of the MACD (or yellow depending on the color of the background screen) is obtained by subtracting the exponential moving average on y days from the moving average on x days

The red line of the MACD is obtained by calculating an exponential moving average on z days of the blue or yellow line.

'X', 'y' and 'z' are the MACD parameters, typically equal each at 12, 26 and 9.

The MACD histogram is obtained by subtracting the red line from the blue or yellow line.

Interpretation:

The MACD is an excellent leading indicator and compensates a part of the delays obtained with the use of simple moving averages.

practical aspect:

There are two main ways to use the MACD:

-The intersections:

A buy signal can be launched when the blue or yellow line crosses below the red line.

A sell signal can be launched when the azzura or yellow line crosses above the red line.

-The differences:

The divergences between the MACD histogram and the price curve identify the tipping points and give more of the strong buying or selling signals.

A bullish divergence is obtained when the stock price reaches a new lower curve while the MACD histogram remains above its previous lowest point.

A bearish divergence is obtained when the curve of the price reaches a new higher while from the MACD histogram remains below its previous highest point.

The bullish or bearish divergences are more significant when held in areas of overbought or oversold.

The signals obtained in the most important time horizons (weekly view, monthly ..) discover the movements of larger prices.

MACD Simplified

Definition:

The normal MACD allows to set the values for

medium 2 while the simplified MACD resumes MACD origin of the formula, which does not work on periods, but on the percentage (in fact corresponds to the average values of 12 333 and 25 666)

In fact, it has percentage = 2 / (nb + 1 period) and it has, therefore, 15% = 2 / (12,333 +1) and 7.5% = 2 / (25,666 + 1)

practical aspect:

This indicator such as MACD, is used in two ways:

Crossroad :

A buy signal is triggered when the blue or yellow line crosses down the red line.

A sell signal is triggered when the blue or yellow line crosses above the red line.

-Divergence:

The divergence between the MACD histogram and the price curve identifies the strong inversion points and thus a strong buy signal or sales.

It is obtained, therefore, a bullish divergence when the price reaches a new minimum curve while the histogram MACD remains higher than its previous minimum.

It is obtained instead a bearish divergence when the price curve reaches a new high while the MACD histogram is less than its previous maximum.

The bullish or bearish divergences are more significant when held in areas of overbought or oversold.

The signals obtained in the most important time frame (for example, weekly or monthly view ..) illustrate the widest price movements.

Mass Index

Definition:

It calculated by the sum of an exponential moving average of the 'range' daily (maximum - minimum).

Mass Index = sum [MME to 9 days of (high-low) /

MME of the MME to 9 days to 9 days of (Max - Min)]

Interpretation:
This indicator allows to reveal a reversal in the trend.
It is based on the price difference between the highest and the lowest. When volatility increases the MASS INDEX increases and when volatility decreases the MASS INDEX decreases.

practical aspect:
The ideal to use this indicator is to tie it to the behavior of an exponential moving average to 9 days applied to quotations.
The indicator MASS INDEX 25 periods becomes interesting when it exceeds upward the horizontal threshold of 27. In this case, you have to wait to come back under the horizontal level of 26.5.
We must therefore observe the behavior of the moving average. If it is oriented upward, a sell signal can announce themselves.

Same if it is oriented downward, a buy signal may appear.

Momentum

Definition:
It is obtained by subtracting the closing 'x' previous days from the end of the day, 'x' being the parameter associated with Momentum.

Interpretation:
E 'an oscillator not limited. It is therefore not a good indicator of overbought / ipervendita.Tuttavia, the passage of 0 gives good buy or sell signals.
It also gives good divergence signals.
A bullish divergence is obtained when the price makes a new low while the Momentum remains below its previous low point.
A bearish divergence is obtained when the curve of prices touching a new higher while the Momentum remains below its previous high point.

Money Flow Index

Definition:

Money Flow = typical price * volume = [(A + B + C) / 3) * volume]

A = max

B = min

C = closing price

Following:

If the typical price typical price of the day before, then Money Flow is a positive flow.

If the typical price <typical price of the day before, then Money Flow is a negative cash flow.

It then calculates the money ratio

MR = (MF + / MF-) with

The MFI can finally be calculated following the formula below:

MFI = 100 - [100 / (1 + MR)]

Interpretation:

The principle is identical to that of the CSR with the parameters of the more volume. If the MFI exceeds 80, the stock is overbought and a decline in prices is expected.

Conversely, if the MFI exceeds the threshold of 20, the stock is in oversold and a recovery should take place.

Volume Index Negative

Definition:
If VOL <VOL (Eve) then NVI = NVI (Eve) + (C - C (Eve)) / [C (Eve) × NVI (Eve)]

If VOL VOL (Eve) then NVI = NVI (previous day)
VOL (previous day) = Volume of the previous day
VOL = Volume of the day
C (Eve) = Quote of the day before

C = Quote of the day
NVI (Eve) = NVI the previous day
NVI: NVI of the day

Interpretation:
The negative volume indicator binds the behavior of volumes than in prices.
It can identify a fall in volumes synchronized to a fall in prices.
The NVI or Negative Volume Indicator identifies only the bearish signals contrary to the indicator of positive volume.
The uninformed investors who follow the trend of rising volumes are purchasing. Conversely, when the volumes are in decline the most informed investors are in the market. The market is quite bullish when the NVI is above its moving average

OBV - On Balance Volume

Definition:
The OBV adds all the volumes of the previous days

where the price closed up compared to the previous day and subtracts all the volumes of the previous regions where prices closed down compared to the previous day.

It remains unchanged when the watertight closing price compared to the eve.

Interpretation:

The OBV should normally follow the same orientation in prices. For this, a divergence allows to anticipate a reversal.

practical aspect:

The OBV gives good divergence signals.

A bullish divergence is obtained when the stock price makes a new low while the TGT remains above its previous lowest point.

A bearish divergence is obtained when the curve of prices touching a new higher while the OBV is below its previous peak.

The Chaikin oscillator

Definition:

Indicator = exponential moving average of x periods of the line of Accumulation / Distribution - Exponential Moving Average of 'y' periods of the line Accumulation / Distribution.

(Default parameters: x = 10 and y = 3)

Interpretation:

This indicator may signal the end of a trend when prices reach a new maximum or minimum while the Chaikin oscillator does not reach a new extreme and changes direction (that corresponds to the divergence with the quotes).

This indicator can be used starting from differences.

practical aspect:

A reversal downward triggered when there is a downward divergence, obtained when the stock price reaches a new low while the indicator remains below its previous minimum.

Price Oscillator

Definition:

Representation in percentage price oscillator

The price oscillator is calculated by subtracting from a short moving average a long.

In its representation as a percentage, the result is divided by the short moving average and multiplied by one hundred.

The parameters are the number of days on which are calculated the 2 moving averages.

Interpretation:

Of the buying or selling signals they can be launched when the oscillator crosses the level 0. The price oscillator works on the same principle MACD where you can parameterize the moving averages. There is also the ability to change the display with a presentation histogram. To do this you must click on the icon to the wrench icon located on the top left of the chart (in the title level). A window (of the property price) appears; It 'just change the style.

Parabolic SAR (On the price)

Definition:

The SAR points are calculated from the price and time.

The parameters are the initial acceleration factor (typically 0.02), the additional factor (such as 0.02) and the limit of the acceleration factor (such as 0.2).

Interpretation:

Points Stop and Reverse are useful to detect trends as they follow the direction of prices.

During a trend, SAR direction is always the same. As long as points remain above or below the price, the trend continues.

practical aspect:

When prices penetrate a point SAR 'stop and reverse', the signal may want to liquidate the present position and possibly take the opposite position. *

Linear Regression Slope

Definition:

This indicator shows the direction of the trend of studying title.

If the indicator passes over the horizontal level 0, the tendency is rather bullish and mutually when the indicator passes below the horizontal level 0 the tendency is rather oriented downward.

More indicator is high and the trend is more pronounced.

practical aspect:

With this indicator, it is suggested to use the R framework that will give you the strength of the trend and confirmation.

Positive Volume Index - PVI

Definition:

If VOL VOL (Eve) then PVI PVI = (eve) + (C - C (Eve)) / [C (Eve) × PVI (Eve)]

If VOL <VOL (Eve) then PVI PVI = (eve)

With:

VOL (Eve) = Volume of Eve

VOL = Volume of the day

C (Eve) = Quote Eve

C = Quote of the day

PVI (Eve) = PVI Eve

PVI PVI = day

Interpretation:

The positive volume indicator binds the behavior of volumes and prices.

It can identify a rise in volumes synchronized to a rise in prices. The Positive Volume Index, or PVI, uniquely identifies the bullish signals contrary all'Indicatore Volume Negative.

Investors inexperienced follow the evolution of rising volumes and position themselves for purchase.

On the contrary, when the volume decreases, more experienced investors entering the market.

The trend is bullish when the two indicators are above their moving average.

Rate of Change - ROC

Definition:
The rate of change divides the price of the day for the price x days before.

Interpretation:
The rate of change is an indicator similar to Momentum.
E 'an overbought / oversold indicator as a function of its position with respect to 100.
also it gives good divergence signals.
A bullish divergence is obtained when the price

makes a new low while the rate of change remains above its previous low point.

A bearish divergence is obtained when the price makes a new high while the rate of change remains below its previous peak.

Price Volume Trend - PVT

Definition:
This indicator is calculated as follows
PVT =% var * Volume + PVT eve
with% var = (eve-closing closure) / chiusuravigilia

Interpretation:
Instead of OBV, the PVT from an idea of the money that flows into and out of a stock. The PVT increases or decreases depending on whether the closing price very various, with important volumes.

practical aspect:
The reversal of bearish trend may trigger a bearish divergence appears. It is obtained when the price

makes a new high or PVT while the indicator remains below its previous peak.

On the contrary, the turnaround to the upside is triggered when there is a bullish divergence. The latter is achieved when the price makes a new low while the PVT indicator remains above its previous low.

Pivots Points

Definition:

The pivot point is calculated as follows

P = (+ Avigilia Bvigilia Cvigilia +) / 3

R2 = P + (Avigilia-Bvigilia)

R1 = 2 * P-Bvigilia

S1 = 2 * P-Avigilia

S2 = P - Avigilia-Bvigilia)

A = max

B = min

C = closure

R2 et resistances R1

S1 and S2 supports.

Interpretation:

This indicator represents the pivot point and two levels of supports and resistances. This indicator lets you know if the price is close to the strategic level and will make you consolidate the gains or take a position in the market.

R-Squared
R^2 or rate of correlation

Definition:

The R-Squared measure the quality of the approximation of a linearee regression curve is used to confirm the trend indicated by the linear regression line itself. Depending on the period used, the R-Squared will be compared to a threshold level 'n'.

practical aspect:

I usually buy signals triggered when crossing the threshold of 30, while sales signals triggered when crossing the threshold of 70.

When the linear regression slope exceeds upward the level 0 (the trend is upward) and R^2 reaches its threshold, the tendency would designate a buy signal as possible.

Linear Regression:

Definition:
The linear regression minimizes the distance between prices and herself.
It is used usually with a channel Raff, compounds of two other straight lines parallel to the regression line, which delimits the quotes.
Interpretation:
The straight line represents the linear regression straight line of equilibrium of the quotations. This feature shows a chart of buyers and sellers involved out of the 'equilibrium price'. The Raff channel shows the extreme prices.
practical aspect:
To view the oscillator linear regression. copy / paste in ProBuilder REM Linear Regression
a = LinearRegression [10] (close)
REM closing price

b = close

REM Oscillator Linear Regression

c = ba

return c

RSI (Relative Strength Index)

Definition:

RSI (on n periods) = 100-100 / (1 + p) with p = (average of the increases on last n periods) / (average reduction on last n periods).

In practice, the more the upward variations are more important the RSI approaching 100, and mutually strong bearish variations approaching 0.

Interpretations:

The RSI is an overbought / oversold indicator. I usually buy signals triggered when you cross the 30 level and sell signals when you cross the level of 70.

The RSI is always between 0 and 100.

practical aspect:

It gives good divergence signals.

A bullish divergence is obtained when the stock price makes a new lower while the RSI remains above its previous lowest point.

A bearish divergence is obtained when the stock price makes a new high while the RSI remains below its previous low.

Repulse

DEFINITION:

The Repulse measure and represents, in the form of the curve, the bullish and bearish thrust contained in each candle.

And 'an auxiliary indicating that it is not associated with changes in the price, in order to make a concrete contribution, as opposed to RSI, MACD and Stochastic. It provides in particular some very valuable information on emotional behavior and stakeholder confidence in the evolution of prices.

practical aspect:

For Futures, a good method is to display on the

same graph the Repulse (1) for examining the tendency to TCT, the Repulse (5) for the CT and the Repulse (15) for the MT. On a 1 minute chart for example, we have in a single glance the validity of the tendency of 1mn, 5mn et 15 mn.

The Repulse gives excellent signals when it slows down to 15, is turned upside down to 5 and diverges to 1, while the trend in progress accelerates and arrives on a support-resistance horizontal. The signals become very strong when they are associated with differences on the indicator Cycles (display in 5mn or 3mn) and to a significant increase in volumes. The success rate becomes very high if more of these signals the quotes out of a trend channel in the direction of the trend itself.

Particularly useful, therefore, of the Repulse allow significantly increase the average gain per trade through optimization of outputs.

practical aspect:

You can enter any of these lines of code in ProBuilder to see the Repulse indicator:

lo = LOWEST [p] (LOW)

hi = HIGHEST [p] (HIGH)

a = 100 * (3 * CLOSE - 2 * lo - OPEN [p-1]) / CLOSE

b = 100 * (OPEN [p-1] + 2 * hi - 3 * CLOSE) / CLOSE

d = ExponentialAverage [5 * p] (a) - EXPONENTIALAVERAGE [5 * p] (b)

RETURN d

In the creation of this indicator, p corresponds to a variable period. We must define it by clicking on (to add) under the heading (indicator parameter).

Scrap type

Definition:

Scrap Type = Square root of [(sum (j = 1 to n) (Closing-MMsemplice on n days) ^{2} / n].

Interpretation:

The standard deviation allows to measure the volatility of the studied title.

It is often linked to the indicators. For example, the Bollinger bands are determined at the base from an arithmetic moving average to which we must draw a higher bandwidth and lower adding and subtracting 2 * (standard deviation).

Stochastic Slow / Fast

DEFINITION:

This oscillator consists of two lines:% K and% D.

It needs three parameters:

- The first parameter is the number of days used in the calculations,

the second is used for the moving average of% K (generalemente 1 for a Fast Stochastic and 3 or 5 for Slow Stochastic),

- the third for the moving average of% D.

Interpretation:

The two lines are oscillators comprised between 0 and 100. The% K indicates the overbought and oversold zones but it is necessary to compare it to the% D because of its high volatility.

practical aspect:

When% K crosses% D upwards, there is a buy signal.

When% K crosses% D downward, there is a sell signal.

The Stocatistici also give right of divergence signals.

You get a bullish divergence when the price makes a new low while the Stochastic remains above its previous low.

You get a bearish divergence when the price makes a new high while the Stochastic remains below its maximum point.

Stochastic smoothed

Definition:

It 'a technical indicator that correlates the closing

quotes with the usual range of the value.

% D or slow stochastic

The calculation of % D is similar to that of fast stochastic, however smoothing allows to obtain a better view.

The formula of D% is the following: % D (y) = 100 * (H (y) / B (y)) with

H (y): the sum of the C - PH (n) on the (x) last days

B (y): the sum of PH (n) - PB (n) on the (x) last days

C: Closing of the day

PB (n): a minimum of n periods

PH (n): a maximum of n times

No: periods

% D Slow is also called moving average of % D

In order to better smooth the results, you can apply an average of % D

Interpretation:

This indicator allows you to identify overbought and oversold levels.

Slow % D, used with % D, will generate buy and sell

signals.

practical aspect:

The title can be considered as oversold if a stochastic (% D or slow% D) is less than 20. To confirm the signal, we should wait for the passing upward of this same level.

The title can be considered as overbought if a stochastic (% D or% D Slow) exceeds 20. To confirm the possible reversal of a bullish trend, one should wait for the downward overcoming of this same level.

A trend bearish reversal may trigger occurs when a bearish divergence. The latter occurs when the stock price makes new highs while the indicator is lower than its previous high.

A bullish reversal trend snaps instead occurs when a bullish divergence. The latter is obtained when the stock price makes a new low while the indicator is higher than its previous minimum.

For the analysis, it is interesting to tie this indicator with other oscillators, such as RSI and MACD, for example.

Stochastic Momentum Oscillator

Definition:

The Stocastic Momentum Oscillator represents the closing position with respect to the midpoint on the contrary of the classical stochastic which represents the closed position with respect to the maximum and minimum. As for the Stocastic Momentum, it applies a double smoothing starting at exponential moving averages.

Interpretation: This is oscillator between -100 and +100.

Its operation is similar to the Stochastic but the supplied signals are more regular.

Its value indicates the overbought zone and is oversold and can use it as a divergence.

practical aspect:

A title can be considered as oversold if a stochastic (% D or% D Slow) passes below the value -40. To confirm the reversal, you have to wait overcoming downward this same level and vice versa.

A reversal of the trend downward is signaled by a bearish divergence, obtained when the stock price makes a new high while the indicator remains below its previous maximum

Conversely, it is in the presence of a turnaround upward when there is a bullish divergence, obtained when the stock price makes a minimum while the indicator remains above its previous minimum.

It may be interesting to tie this indicator with other oscillators, such as the R Squared (confirming trends).

SuperTrend

SuperTrend was developed by Oliver Seban. This indicator has the advantage of running on all scales of time and on all media. You can make use of it on the stock, futures or forex, is in 5min is weekly. And 'the ideal tool to accompany trends and optimize the outputs. The SuperTrend evolves above or below the prices and is linked to the type of trend. Use particularly the closure of the day to filter out false signals that can appear during periods without trend. The SuperTrend is calculated from a coefficient applied to the average volatility of the last candles (or bar chart according to the type of rapresentazione chosen). We suggest to use the coefficients 3:10 for the multiplier and the number of bars. Of identical form to the SAR Wilder; SuperTrend the following prices as a STOP (using the most appropriate calculations to volatility) with the difference that does not change the values in periods without trend. It allows you to give more space and time for the price to enter the trend and discover the most important movements. In a general way, the signal is interpreted as good a bullish signal when the SuperTrend is below the price and bearish when the SuperTrend is higher than the price.

TEMA - Triple Exponential Moving Average:

Definition:

It is estimated in a first MME1 time, the days an exponential moving average on the closing prices. As a result, it is estimated MME2, the moving average of days an exponential MME1
then calculates MME3, an exponential moving average days MME2
He finally gets the indicator TEMA = 2 * MME2 - MME3

Details:

The TEMA is a combination of three exponential moving averages. Note the parameter p THEME:
THEME = 3 * (mm1 - mm2) + mm3 with
mm1 = exponential moving average of the closing quotation (by default) and parameter p
mm2 = Exponential Moving Average of mm1 and parameter p
mm3 = mm2 Exponential Moving Average and parameter p

Interpretation:
This indicator is faster and more smoothed moving average of a standard. The TEMA as the DEMA can be used in place of moving averages or applied on other indicators such as the MACD, the oscillatoristocastici.

TRIX

Definition:
This indicator is obtained in two stages.
The first consists in calculating the exponential moving average of 3 triple period starting from the closing prices.
After calculating the third moving average, calculating the standard deviation as a percentage of the quotes of this average, you get the TRIX.

Interpretation:
The TRIX is an indicator that evolves close to the line 0.
E'sovente used with its moving average smoothing

period 9.

As a MACD and its moving average, TRIX and its average ideal to discover the entry and exit points. practical aspect:

When the TRIX (black line) crosses from below its moving average (red dotted line), can trigger a buy signal.

Conversely, when the TRIX (black line) crosses above its moving average (red dotted line) a sales signale can shoot.

The TRIX is a indicatote that gives some interesting signals in a trending market.

Percentage variation

Definition:

The percentage change is calculated by determining the percentage of each day of the closing price change compared to the previous day. The moving average is the average of the percentage changes over the last x days.

Enter the number 0 or leave empty the box of the

parameter associated to not display this moving average.

Interpretation:
This indicator highlights the current volatility of the value and compares it with the previous periods.

Volume Oscillator

Definition:
To calculate this indicator, two averages of volume furniture is sufficient to calculate on two different periods of time. The volume oscillator is uo 'express in the form of percentage change% = 100 * [(short average volume - long average volume) / (volume average long)]

Interpretation:
The interest of this is an indicator of whether the underlying trend volumes are growing or not.
practical aspect:
For the same principle of crossing two moving

averages, when the average short passes over the long average, the oscillator becomes positive and vice versa.

In a bullish movement, a normal situation shows that when the share price increases, that the volume oscillator becomes positive. Similarly, in a downward movement, a fall in prices is accompanied by a decrease of the oscillator volume.

Volumes Spectrum

And 'possible to highlight the cumulative volume for each level of the value for money.
You may also define the number of bars visible by changing the value of the associated parameter.

Volume Rate Of Change

Definition:
The principle of the calculation is the same as that of ROC but calculated on the volume. The VROC

divides the volume of the day with the volume of 'x' days

Interpretation:
Show the volume change rate. Of the purchase of entry points they can be highlighted when coping with resistance occurring on the indicator. It 'also can use the bullish or bearish divergences.

Williams'% R

Definition:
It is the ((highest periods of the n-current shutdown) / (maximum of n-periods of minimum periods n)) * (- 100).
The parameter is the number of days used in the calculations of% R

Interpretation:
Williams'% R is an overbought / oversold indicator.

practical aspect:

E 'between 0 and -100.

The values -80 and -20 can be used as a limit to locate the overbought / oversold situations. However, it is better to wait for a change in price direction can be detected, for example, with MACD before buying or selling. Note that when% R forms a peak and tips, you can 'wait to fall in price.

Accumulation Williams.

Definition:

TRH = the greater value between (the closing of the eve or the top of the day)

TRL = the lower value between (the closing of the eve or the low of the day)

If closing of the closing day of the vigil then A / D = Closing of the day-TRL

If closing the day <closing the Eve then A / D = Closing of the day-TRH

If closing the day = Closing eve A / D = 0

A / D = William A / D Day + A / D eve.

Interpretation:

The accumulation corresponds to a market dominated by buyers, while the distribution corresponds to a market dominated by venditori.Questo indicator is mainly used starting from differences.

practical aspect:
It occurs a reversal downward when you see a bearish divergence. This is achieved when the price makes a new high and the A / D fails to make new highs.
It verificaun reversal to the upside when it appears a bullish divergence. This is achieved when the price makes a new low and the A / D fails to make new lows.

ZigZag indicator

Definition:

The Zig-Zag indicator is made up of straight slope that change when a change occurs on the higher prices to the amount specified (in percentage or absolute terms).

Interpretation:
The Zig-Zag indicator only represents the most interesting movements excluding the slightest movement. A parameter allows you to choose the desired sensitivity.
The last point representative of the indicator can be changed in the light of future prices.

practical aspect:
It can be very useful to break down the evolution of a security in the form of Elliott waves.

www.ingramcontent.com/pod-product-compliance
Lightning Source LLC
Chambersburg PA
CBHW021436210526
45463CB00002B/535